CLASS 142

CLASS 142
THE BUS THAT BECAME A TRAIN

MARTYN HILBERT

FONTHILL

Fonthill Media Language Policy

Fonthill Media publishes in the international English language market. One language edition is published worldwide. As there are minor differences in spelling and presentation, especially with regard to American English and British English, a policy is necessary to define which form of English to use. The Fonthill Policy is to use the form of English native to the author. Martyn Hilbert was born and educated in England; therefore, British English has been adopted in this publication.

Fonthill Media Limited
Fonthill Media LLC
www.fonthill.media
office@fonthillmedia.com

First published in the United Kingdom and the United States of America 2020

British Library Cataloguing in Publication Data:
A catalogue record for this book is available from the British Library

Copyright © Martyn Hilbert 2020

ISBN 978-1-78155-823-2

The right of Martyn Hilbert to be identified as the author of this work has been asserted by him in accordance with the Copyright, Designs and Patents Act 1988.

All rights reserved. No part of this publication may be reproduced, stored in a retrieval system or transmitted in any form or by any means, electronic, mechanical, photocopying, recording or otherwise, without prior permission in writing from Fonthill Media Limited

Typeset in 10pt on 13pt Sabon
Printed and bound in England

Contents

Introduction   7

1   In the Beginning   9
2   The 142/0s: 142001–142050   20
3   The 142/1s: 142051–142096   25
4   Into Service   28
5   Newton Heath Depot Maintenance   38
6   At Work   42
7   Interiors   82
8   A 142 Miscellany   88
9   Scale Models   93

Bibliography   96

Introduction

The ninety-six members of the Class 142 Pacer Train fleet were the marriage of Leyland National bus and railway technology to produce a cheap solution to replace some of the ageing, worn-out, BR first-generation diesel multiple unit fleet in the mid-1980s. With an envisaged life span of around ten years, they were intended as a 'stop-gap' until something better could be afforded. In the event, much of the fleet has lasted almost thirty-five years, and despite much re-engineering during their lifetime, the Class 142s have been the backbone of many services across the UK railway network. When new, they presented a bright, clean, fresh image compared to what had gone before, and they were welcomed by passengers, user-groups, and staff alike. Like all rolling stock, the time has finally come for these unsung workhorses, the design failing to meet the Persons of Reduced Mobility Regulations (PRM-TSI), and subsequently, in 2019, fleet withdrawals commenced. Having been part of the railway landscape in the north-west, Cumbria, the north-east, Yorkshire, the south-west, Lincolnshire, and South Wales, they have gone about their daily business unnoticed; only when they are gone will they be missed. In the following ninety-six pages, I have tried to give a background to how the Class 142s came about, their life and times in words and pictures, and an insight into the maintenance programme that kept the Northern fleet running. For completeness, there is a summary and listing of scale models produced. Fortunately, I photographed members of the fleet from new, and the selection of images show them in their early years and liveries, through to their twilight period in various locations nationwide. Living in the north-west, with my home close to the East Lancashire route, and with the Class 142s visible from our house on a daily basis, I felt that their passing needed to be commemorated, resulting in the words you are now reading. The book is intended to be an informative read, and not a technical treatise.

The compilation of a book is a team effort. Once again, my thanks go to Alan Sutton and the team at Fonthill Media for having the faith in me and allowing another selection of my work to appear in print. Thank you to my wife, Gillian, and to friends and photographers John Sloane and Roger Sutcliffe for their support. Thanks to Arriva Northern and in particular Phil Robinson, shift production manager, and his team at Newton Heath depot, for access and information on their 142 fleet. Thank you to John

Class 142

Baker for information and anecdotes from when the 142s were new, thanks to the Wensleydale Railway and the Whitrope Heritage Centre for access to LEV1 and RB004 respectively, and finally, I wonder if the design team at British Leyland and BR ever imagined that the trains they designed and produced 'on the cheap' in the early 1980s would still be in daily service in the second decade of the twenty-first century, and that one would become an exhibit at the National Railway Museum for future generations to admire.

Martyn Hilbert
Lostock Hall, Preston, Lancashire
July 2020

A newly delivered 142034 in BR Provincial Services blue livery was stabled at Preston during crew training duties on 2 March 1986.

1

In the Beginning

In the past, before nationalisation of the railway system in January 1948, various attempts with railbuses had been tried out, with little success. In the early days of British Railways, a trial had been carried out with an ACV/BUT (A.C. Vehicles/British United Traction) demonstration railbus/railcar that had three small lightweight vehicles that could be operated in tandem, or singly. Known as the 'Flying Brick' and with bodywork by Park Royal, they were eventually given BR numbers (M79740–42). A further eight cars (M79743–50) were delivered between 1955 and 1957, though the cars were not particularly successful or reliable, and all had been withdrawn by 1961; all were scrapped at Derby in 1963.

As part of the British Railways 1955 Modernisation Plan, orders would be placed with BR workshops and private contractors to build 4,600 diesel multiple unit (DMU) vehicles. In the late 1950s, in an attempt to reduce rural branch line costs, and with an eye on German (DB) railway practice, twenty-two lightweight diesel railbuses were ordered from five different manufacturers.

Builder	Fleet Numbers	Number Built	Introduced	Seats
A.C. Cars Ltd.	79975–79979	5	1958	46
Park Royal.	79970–79974	5	1958	50
D. Wickham.	79965–79969	5	1958	48
Waggon and Maschinenbau	79960–79964	5	1958	56
Bristol/Eastern Coach Works	79958 and 79959	2	1958	56

Mostly delivered from 1958 onwards, in many instances, they operated on branch lines that were still fully staffed (stations, signal boxes, permanent way staff, etc.), so although the operational cost of the railbuses was effective (even with two crew

Class 142

A British Railways railbus, one of five built by the Waggon and Maschinenbau Company of Germany in 1958, E79960 (now preserved), was running along the Ribble Steam Railway at Preston Docks on 6 October 2013. The compact railbus had seats for fifty-six passengers.

In refurbished BR white with blue stripe livery, a Metro-Cammell Class 101 formed of cars E50214 and E53141 stood at Selby with a Leeds–Hull service on 12 September 1981. The well-built Metro-Cammell DMUs were the subject of mid-life refurbishment, and the last of the type would not be withdrawn until 2003.

In the Beginning

members), they were put to work on lines that could not make a profit. In Germany, their railbuses had unpowered trailers, with the ability to increase the seating capacity as demand required, giving greater flexibility of operation. Unfortunately, the BR railbuses were all individually powered vehicles and could not work in multiple; consequently, on lines where traffic increased because of their introduction, they were a victim of their own success due to limited seating capacity and were replaced by conventional DMUs. The 'Beeching Plan' of 1963 also sowed the seeds of their demise; much of the rural network that the railbuses were designed for would be erased from the map by the late 1960s. Subsequently, the last of the BR railbuses would be withdrawn from passenger use in 1968.

Most railway rolling stock has a fatigue life of around forty years, and with the last of the BR first-generation DMU fleet having been introduced in 1963, by the mid-1970s, thought was being given as what to do with the ageing fleet. A Metro-Cammell 3-Car Class 101 set was given a trial refurbishment in 1975 (Cars 51451, 59545, and 51589), with each car having differing degrees of improvements/upgrades, dependant on costing. In its then startling white with blue stripe livery, the unit made a nationwide tour to demonstrate what could be done with the best of the existing fleet. Cost restraints would eventually see only a small proportion of the DMU fleet refurbished, but the fact remained that the remaining cars were getting older, becoming old-fashioned in the eyes of the travelling public, proving less reliable and economical to maintain; replacement would be necessary by the 1980s.

A possible solution came about in 1982, when BREL (British Rail Engineering Ltd) unveiled two demonstrator Class 210 DEMUs: 210001 was a four-car set and 210002 was made up of three cars. Both were constructed at BREL Litchurch Lane at Derby, 210001 was fitted with a Paxman 1,125-hp engine and 210002 with a 1,140-hp MTU engine. No. 210001 was designed as an 'outer-suburban' unit and fitted with first- and second-class accommodation, while 210002 was a 'suburban' unit and was second class only. Looking similar to a Bedford–St Pancras Class 317 electric multiple unit, the pair of units made various trials and passenger runs across the network. With their above-floor-mounted engines, located in a compartment behind the driving cab at one end of the units (similar to existing DEMUs on the Southern Region of BR), they were well-received. Unfortunately, they came at a cost—around £1 million for a four-car set, and at a time when spending on BR was restricted and the government of the day was looking forwards to possible privatisation of the entire BR network, the Class 210 project went no further.

In the late 1970s, the Railway Technical Centre (RTC) at Derby had been experimenting with high-speed running using a four-wheel chassis as part of the advanced passenger train (APT) project. This chassis would eventually be fitted with bodywork of a Leyland National bus, supplied by the truck and bus division of British Leyland. While the single car was initially unpowered, it would eventually become a powered vehicle after being fitted with a Leyland TL10 205-hp underfloor diesel engine. It was christened LEV1 (Leyland Experimental Vehicle 1) and given the BR departmental number RDB975874.

The Leyland National single-deck bus, which was a collaboration between British Leyland and the National Bus Company (NBC), was manufactured between 1972 and 1985 and constructed at a specially built assembly plant at Lillyhall, Workington, Cumbria. The bodywork was integral, constructed of aluminium alloy, and made of

Class 142

The BREL Class 210 prototype 210002, a three-car set powered by a MTU 1,140-hp diesel engine mounted above the floor, was departing from Reading in September 1986. (*Courtesy John Sloane*)

Part of the large fleet of Ribble, Leyland National Mk I, NTC 625M Fleet Number 445 that had been new in August 1973, stood between duties at Preston Bus Station in August 1980. The Mk I Nationals were produced from 1972 until 1978.

In the Beginning

A former British Airways Leyland National Mk 2, B361 LOY, a dual-door version dating from 1985, has been preserved. The Mk 2 version of the National was produced between 1978–1985, and the bus shown here was among the last of the type built.

sections, riveted together, each being 1,421 mm in length and 2,500 mm in width, which gave a modular construction. Both single- and dual-door versions were available. The interior fittings were all very much clip/screw and prefabricated parts that eased assembly, negating the need for specialist coachbuilding skills in their construction. The vehicles became a familiar sight the length and breadth of the UK, with all of the large operators having sizable fleets, including London Transport. Made in two versions—Mk 1 (1972–1978) and Mk 2 (1978–1985)—it was a highly successful design with over 7,000 vehicles being produced, the last examples of which lasted in timetabled, normal daily use until 2007.

With LEV1, here was a possible solution to the replacement of some of the BR first-generation DMU fleet. The prototype made visits across the British Rail network to assess its suitability. In 1980, LEV1 was sent to the United States for a period of trials, with an eye to possible export sales. It returned to the UK in 1986. Meanwhile, a consortium had been formed between British Rail and British Leyland, 'Associated Rail Technologies' (ART) in 1982 with a view to moving the railbus project forwards.

With LEV1 being 8 m in length and seating only thirty passengers, an extended version (at 15.3 m in length, assembled by the Wickham Company in Hertfordshire, and made specifically for the US market), LEV2, was unveiled in 1980. Following trials in

Class 142

Above: LEV1 (RDB975874) was the first attempt at second-generation railbus technology and was built in 1978. Now part of the NRM collection, it was stored at the Wensleydale Railway on 9 October 2018.

Left: The front end of LEV1 (RDB975874), clearly showing the standard Leyland National bus cab front that was utilised at both ends of the railbus.

In the Beginning

the United States, it would eventually be sold to Amtrack. Unfortunately, the hoped-for export orders never materialised.

Back in the UK, another prototype, R3, was produced by BREL/BL in 1981. RDB977020 was 15.3 m in length and was again trialled on various routes, including the Severn Beach branch in Bristol. It was re-gauged to 5 feet 3 inches and sold to Northern Ireland Railways in 1982. One of the issues facing the adoption of the prototypes on the UK network was the cab construction. It was felt at the time that the standard bus cab end was unable to provide sufficient protection in the event of a collision. The compressive force when a collision occurs would not only damage the cab area, but unless there is sufficient resistance in place, the bodywork (and passengers) would be compromised. With this in mind, ART produced a two-car Class 140 prototype in 1981. Having Leyland National bodywork but with cabs that were derived from the Class 317 EMU, the unit was fitted with high-backed seating (the previous prototypes had retained the simple bench-like bus seats) and a single lavatory. No. 140001 (cars 55500 and 55501) was an ugly-looking beast, but it went on a nationwide tour in 1981–1983 to assess its suitability. It was given a mixed reception; while it resembled a conventional train, many thought that the 'cheap and cheerful' railbus concept had been so diluted and over-engineered that they asked 'why not build replacement conventional DMU vehicles?' The unit rode well enough on welded track, but with a top speed of 75 mph, the ride could become lively and noisy at speed on a conventional jointed track. Each car was powered by a Leyland 200-hp TL11 engine and had self-changing gears (SCG) gearboxes with Gmeinder final drive to one axle on each car.

A pristine-looking R3 railbus (RDB977020) was stood outside the BREL works at Litchurch Lane, Derby, when new in 1981. (*Courtesy John Sloane*)

Class 142

The prototype Class 140 two-car railbus, 140001, was arriving at Bamber Bridge with the 12.46 Colne to Preston service on a damp 28 September 1981. The unit was being trialled across the BR network on various routes to assess its capability and passenger reaction. The Class 317 EMU-type cab front was a major step-change from the other previous railbus prototypes that had the standard Leyland National bus front end.

Following the trials with 140001, the West Yorkshire Passenger Transport Executive (WYPTE) ordered twenty two-car railbuses in 1984. The Class 141 fleet (141001–141020) again featured Leyland National bodywork, but with a simplified and much more aesthetic cab design. Each car had the same Leyland TL11 engine under the floor, and they were fitted with SCG gearboxes and Gmeinder final drives as per the Class 140 prototype. The standard bus body was retained, and with 'two plus two' bus-type seating, they appeared very cramped internally. The narrowness of the body (2,500 mm) also created a gap between station platform edges and the entrance doors. No. 141001 was initially turned out in conventional BR blue and grey, the blue shade being 'Barrow Corporation' blue, as the Leyland factory in Cumbria had no standard rail blue, the Barrow shade being the nearest they had to hand. The first five units would be initially finished in blue and grey, but eventually, 141002–141020 were finished in WYPTE livery (as applied to their bus fleet); being a striking buttermilk and Verona green, they made a visual impact on a network that at the time was in corporate rail blue. While they brought a fresh look to the services they operated, the fleet became unreliable and would eventually be reworked in 1988/89, with all twenty units then being finished in the revised WYPTE livery of red and cream. They were finally retired from service in 1997. Twelve units were exported to Iran in 2001–02, with two other to the Netherlands in 2003.

In the Beginning

The Class 140 prototype, 140001, and the first of the West Yorkshire Class 141 units, 141001, were stood side-by-side at Leeds Holbeck depot on 15 March 1987.

In West Yorkshire PTE Verona green and buttermilk livery, 141010 was stood at Leeds with a service to Knottingley on 20 October 1987. The narrow bus body at 2,500 mm used on the 141s gave a gap between the side of the bodywork and the station platforms, as clearly shown here.

17

Class 142

In the Beginning

In 1984, ART also constructed a Class 141-type two-car unit, specifically for export trials. It was metre gauge, and the unit was shipped out to Malaysia and Thailand, also visiting Indonesia. Again, there were no follow-on orders. A pair of standard-gauge single units were also constructed in 1984. RB002 had Class 141-type cab ends and was sent to Sweden, Denmark, and the Netherlands for trials, eventually having trials in Canada. RB002 eventually returned to the UK in 1992, having the ignominy of being used as an office at Litchurch Lane for a period, before being preserved in 1998 and ending up in a private collection in Northern Ireland.

RB004 was a similar vehicle, fitted with US-type knuckle couplings, with a bell fitted to each cab front, again with prospects for export orders which in the event never materialised. RB004 was trialled in the United States in 1984, where, besides running trials with various US railroads, it was also exhibited at the Washington International Exhibition of Transportation Systems. The unit was shipped back to the UK in 1986. RB004 survives in preservation at the Whitrope Heritage Centre, based on the former Waverley Route in the Borders Region of Southern Scotland.

Opposite above: Following on from the production of the Class 141 fleet, two single-car prototypes were built in 1984. This is RB004, a double-ended railbus with a centre-driving position and small doors adjacent to the cab end that could enable the driver to collect fares and issue tickets as per a bus. Complete with its integral bell on the cab ends, RB004 was demonstrated in the United States and is now preserved at the Whitrope Heritage Centre seen here on 13 April 2019.

Opposite below: The rather Spartan interior of prototype railbus RB004 that was built in 1984. Complete with 'two plus two' Leyland National bus seating, the rear of the centre driving position is at the far end of the body. This view emphasises the narrow body at 2,500 mm in width, as per the bus. RB004 has two small passenger saloons either side of a central double door, the total seating capacity being twenty-eight.

2

The 142/0s: 142001–142050

Following the delivery of the twenty Class 141s, British Rail ordered a further batch of units, which became the first batch of Class 142s. Following criticism of the narrow body used in the 141s, and the subsequent gap between the station platform edge and the sides of the bodywork, ART revised the body design and jigs at the Workington factory and added a further 300 mm to widen the body modules, giving a total width of 2,800 mm compared to the 141s at 2,500 mm. The upside of this design tweak enabled not only a reduction of the gap between the unit and the platform edge, but also allowed the interior to have a 'three plus two' seating configuration—a 20 per cent increase on the seating capacity of each unit (121) compared with a Class 141 (94).

To fit the widened bodyshells, a revised cab design was designed and used on the new units. The order was for fifty two-car sets, numbered 142001–142050, comprising of a driving motor second (DMS) and a driving motor second lavatory (DMSL). They were all fitted with Leyland TL11 205-hp diesel engines beneath each car, each with 125-gallon fuel tanks, and had standard Leyland National bus-type seating and a top speed of 75 mph. At the cab ends, they were fitted with BSI Tightlock couplers, and the two cars were fitted back-to-back with a gangway connection and an inner bar coupling. Each two-car set had a price tag of £350,000. Each car was fitted with Deans folding double doors as per the road vehicles and had cable-operated hydraulic braking systems, SCG gearboxes, and Gmeinder final drive to the rear axle of each car.

Each bodyshell was completed at Workington and then sent by road to BREL Litchurch Lane at Derby, where the bodies were attached to the steel chassis and the cars were fitted out internally. At one end near the entrance doors, one car had a small longitudinal saloon with a lockable door, so that parcels and mail could be carried at one end securely. The sets were finished in three different liveries, reflecting their sphere of operation.

Nos 142001–142014 were finished in Greater Manchester PTE (GMPTE) orange and brown livery, 142015–142027 were in a pseudo-GWR-style chocolate and cream livery for use in Devon and Cornwall, while the remainder, 142028–142050, were completed in BR Provincial Services two-tone blue livery. With an eye to the future, the last unit completed (142050) was fitted with Voith hydraulic transmission rather than the SCG mechanical gearbox arrangement that had been fitted as standard to all the railbuses produced since LEV1.

Following some trial running around the Derby area, the first orange Greater Manchester units were delivered to Newton Heath depot in East Manchester in June and July 1985. The first passenger use appeared to be on 14 September 1985, when 142001 and 142003 were utilised on a staff excursion from Manchester Victoria to Blackpool North. When officially launched at Manchester Victoria on 2 September 1985, the fleet was christened with the name 'Pacer'—a title that has stuck. The Newton Heath units first entered regular timetabled operation on 30 September 1985.

The thirteen Devon and Cornwall sets (142015–142027) were sent new to Plymouth Laira depot, where, after driver training, they were utilised on the Barnstaple, Exmouth, and Paignton branches, with use on stopping services on the west of England main line between Exeter and Newton Abbot. In Cornwall, they replaced first-generation DMUs on the Falmouth, Gunnislake, Looe, Newquay, and St Ives branches. With twelve diagrams to operate and with only one unit spare daily, the thirteen members of the fleet were intensively used. Due to the maritime connotations with the Cornish branches, the units were given the 'Skipper' fleet name. The remaining twenty-two Provincial-liveried sets were divided between Newton Heath depot and Neville Hill depot at Leeds.

The first of the Class 142 fleet, 142001, in Greater Manchester PTE orange and brown livery, was stood at Preston on 17 October 1987.

Class 142

Devon and Cornwall livered 142025 and 142027 were arriving at Starcross with the 16.35 Paignton to Exmouth service on 24 May 1987.

No. 142037 was departing from Croston with the 17.25 Ormskirk to Preston service on 21 May 1986. The Preston–Ormskirk route had gone over to 100 per cent new Pacer operation from 7 April 1986.

The 142/0s: 142001–142050

The penultimate Class 142, 142049, was sent to Canada when new and was an exhibit at expo86 in Vancouver. It also was trialled with VIA Rail and ran on the British Columbia Railway. No. 142049 returned home in pristine condition in 1987, becoming part of the Newton Heath allocation of 142s. The smart-looking 142049, fresh from its transatlantic exploits, was passing Farington Curve Junction with a Preston to Clitheroe special on 11 July 1987.

The last of the first batch of Class 142s, 142050, was fitted with Voith hydraulic transmission from new, as a precursor to how the rest of the fleet would be eventually equipped. When built, it was a one-off mechanically and was at Bamber Bridge with a Colne to Preston service on 7 July 1987.

Class 142

The introduction of the 142s enabled many of the then well-worn first-generation DMUs to be finally withdrawn. At the time (1985–86), those units appeared to be from another age, while the new 142 fleet gave the travelling public a bright and clean image. As an example, the Preston to Ormskirk line went over to 100 per cent Pacer operation on 7 April 1986; the local rail user group (OPTA) welcomed the fact the 'their' line was a recipient of the new trains. An additional bonus for BR was that the new trains were 25 per cent more fuel-efficient than the units they were replacing. The penultimate unit built (142049) did not enter service when new but was shipped to Canada to be an exhibit at expo86 in Vancouver. Following its exposure at the exhibition, 142049 was trialled with Canadian operator VIA Rail as well as demonstration runs on the British Columbia Railway; it was eventually shipped back to the UK in 1987, when the immaculate unit took up its duties working from Newton Heath depot in Manchester.

3

The 142/1s: 142051–142096

As production and delivery of the first fifty Class 142s was still underway, in 1986, BR Provincial Services ordered another forty-five × two-car Class 142s; they became known as Class 142/1s. The original intention was to number them 142151–142196, but in the event, the number sequence followed directly on from the first batch, and they were given the set numbers 142051–142096. All forty-five were finished in BR Provincial two-tone blue livery. They appeared identical to the earlier built 142s, but with exception of the first of the batch (142051), externally, the roof sections on the newer versions had three reinforcing ribs running longitudinally along the roof, while the earlier batch had a multi-ribbed roof section. Commensurate with the 142/0s, one car was a Driving Motor Second (DMS) and one was was a Driving Motor Second Lavatory (DMSL), both cars being 15.5 m (51 feet) in length, with the DMS weighing in at 24.5 tonnes and the DMSL weighing 25 tonnes.

Significantly, the 142/1s would be the last railbuses supplied to British Rail that were built by the ART consortium. The first 142/1 (142051) was delivered to Newton Heath depot in April 1986, and final example (142096) went new to Neville Hill depot in June 1987. All were supplied with the same equipment, fittings, and engines as per the Class 142/0 fleet.

Class 142

The first of the second batch of Class 142s (142/1), 142051 was stood at Lostock Hall with a Preston to Colne service on 11 March 1987. This view shows that 142051 had the same multi-ribbed roof as per 142001–142050. From 142052 onwards, the roof section was formed of three longitudinal ribs.

As 142035 and 142064 were passing at Lostock Hall, the different roof sections between a 142/0 (142035) and a 142/1 (142064) were clearly visible. No. 142035 has a multi-ribbed roof section, while 142064 has the three longitudinal ribs along the roof. Only 142051 of the 142/1 batch had the earlier type roof.

The 142/1s: 142051–142096

Brand new Class 142/1s 142077 and 142078 were stabled at Leeds Neville Hill depot on 15 March 1987. A solitary Class 141 was stood in the background.

A new-looking 142096 was stood at Croston with the 17.25 Ormskirk to Preston service on 5 August 1987. No. 142096 was the last of the forty-six Class 142/1s and the last ever railbus built by the (BR/British Leyland) ART consortium.

4

Into Service

With a fleet of ninety-six bright new units, the 142s became a familiar sight across the country. However, within weeks of their introduction, the fleet was starting to have some reliability issues. The Deans folding double doors, which had performed well on the road vehicles, were causing problems due to not locating correctly when in the closed position, creating delays and failures, as if the doors were not closed properly, the braking system would not allow the unit to move. Additionally, the SCG mechanical gearboxes, which had been a standard fitment to not only the Leyland National bus but also to all the prototypes and the Class 141 fleet, appeared to be not robust enough for the hurly-burly of railway operation. The cable-actuated braking systems were also found to be ineffective and caused problems when the cables stretched with use.

To add to the mounting catalogue of problems, in February 1987, Leyland announced that they were ceasing production of the TL11 engine, which would eventually make the 192 power units fitted under the Class 142 fleet obsolete. BR faced so many issues that many 142s were put in storage, and after much transferring and cobbling together, surviving first-generation DMUs were brought into service to keep things running. With much of the traditional DMU fleet gone, there was no option but to bring locomotive-hauled services on certain routes, a decision that delighted many enthusiasts at the time, bringing the sight of loco-hauled trains back to lines and areas where they had not been seen for many years.

In the West Country, issues with excessive tyre and flange wear on the wheelsets of the thirteen 'Skipper' units became a major problem. When the fleet was in use on some of the tightly curved Cornish branches, the spacing between the wheels of the four-wheel chassis was not only causing wear to the wheelsets and track, but also excessive flange squealing—a fact not appreciated by residents who lived close to the railway. Despite some perseverance at Laira depot and the installation of flange lubrication equipment on the worst of the sharp curves, it was eventually decided to throw in the towel; in 1988, the West Country sojourn of the Class 142 'Skippers' was over. The thirteen-strong fleet was transferred north to the Newton Heath and Heaton depots, where their chocolate and cream livery made them look out of place. With no internet, etc. in those days, no one in the enthusiast world knew that these units were being transferred. I well remember the total surprise when a Skipper worked a Colne to Blackpool South service one summer afternoon in 1988.

Into Service

Still carrying its Devon and Cornwall GWR-inspired chocolate and cream livery, 'Skipper' 142024 was stood on the up slow line at Leyland with the 10.00 Preston to Liverpool Lime Street service on 7 September 1991. The unit has had a small Newton Heath depot sticker (complete with Lancashire Witch) added below the cab windows.

With over half the fleet stored in 1987, it was decided to rework the fleet to improve reliability and iron out some inherent design issues. The Coventry-made self-changing gears (SGC) gearboxes were replaced by Voith T211r hydraulic transmissions, as per the original fitment to 142050. The folding doors were also replaced with a more robust and reliable twin-leaf, inward-pivoting version that located correctly when in the closed position. The unreliable and potentially dangerous cable-actuated braking system was also replaced with conventional air brakes. From 1993 onwards, the entire fleet was progressively re-engined with a Cummins LT10-R six-cylinder diesel engine rated at 225 hp, with the last examples being re-engined in 1996.

With the former 'Skipper' units absorbed into the provincial services operations, members of the fleet would become a familiar sight across the north-west, Cumbria, the north-east, Yorkshire, and Lincolnshire on a variety of routes and services. Their BSI Tightlock Couplers enabled the 142s to work in multiple with most of the BR second-generation DMUs (Classes 150/1, 150/2, 153, 155, 156, and 158), which would often see the fleet performing some longer-distance runs.

On 5 October 1991, an incident at Edge Hill, Liverpool, saw the first of the 142s to be withdrawn from service. Following braking problems due to debris on the track following some vandalism while running between Manchester and Liverpool, 142059 ran out of control down the incline from Edge Hill to Liverpool Lime Street station. Fortunately, the service had been terminated and there were no passengers on board, and the crew managed to escape without injury, Lime Street station being evacuated before the errant unit hit the hydraulic buffer stop at the end of the line on platform four. Car 55755 left the rails, rearing-up over the buffers, the front of the unit coming to rest against a steel roof support, the car breaking its back in the process. The other car (55709) was not so severely damaged and for a time languished at Newton Heath depot before being scrapped.

As time passed, BR Provincial services became Regional Railways with its own identity and livery, as a prelude to eventual privatisation of the UK network. In 1992, seventeen Newton Heath units (142041–142049 and 142051–142058) were refurbished for the Merseyside Passenger Transport Executive (MPTE), primarily for use on Merseyrail City Line workings from Liverpool Lime Street. They were fitted with 'three plus two' individual low-backed seating, yellow and grey interior fittings and had their original cab front destination display replaced by a dot-matrix arrangement. They were all repainted in a striking yellow Merseyrail corporate livery.

The fourteen Greater Manchester units (142001–142014) would also lose their original orange and brown livery in this period, in favour of a revised GMPTE scheme of grey and white with an orange bodyside stripe. Another livery variant was the application of Tyne and Wear PTE yellow to some of the fleet that had gravitated north to Heaton depot. One problem with the application of dedicated area liveries was that despite careful diagramming and planning, units tended to be 'common user' and a Greater Manchester-liveried 142 could be seen working in Cumbria, while a Merseyrail example could be found plying its trade in East Lancashire.

In 1999, another incident would see another member of the Class 142 fleet 'bite the dust'. Units 142008 and 142003 were running empty stock from Crewe to Liverpool Lime Street on 23 June, when the two units were routed into the Down Loop at Winsford

Resplendent in newly applied BR Regional Railways livery, 142033 was stood at Bamber Bridge with the 15.08 Blackpool South to Colne service on 25 August 1995.

Into Service

In Merseytravel livery, branded 'Regional Railways' 142052 was stood in the north-facing bay platform at Lancaster with the 15.58 departure to Morecambe on 15 June 1996.

Carrying the revised Greater Manchester PTE livery, 142006 was passing Kirkham North Junction while working a Blackpool North–Manchester Victoria service on 3 March 1997. All the Greater Manchester 142s (142001–142014) were re-liveried into this revised scheme.

Class 142

A pair of former Devon and Cornwall 'Skippers', 142018 and 142021, were stood at Ruswarp with a Whitby-bound service on 15 July 1997. Both units are in Tyne and Wear PTE livery. (*Courtesy Roger Sutcliffe*)

on the WCML. Unfortunately, the pair of units overran the red signal protecting the junction at the north end of the loop, running through the points and onto the WCML. The 06.15 London Euston to Glasgow Central Virgin Trains service, hauled by Class 87 electric loco 87027 'Wolf of Badenoch', had to make an emergency brake application, nevertheless striking the rear car of 142008 at approximately 20 mph. The driver of 87027 escaped injury, and no passengers on the Virgin service were injured, but the front of the Class 87 ripped open the aluminium alloy body of 142008, and the front of 87027 was embedded in the rear cab and saloon area. It was indeed fortunate that the 142s were running empty stock. Needless to say, 142008 was a write-off and became the second member of the class to be withdrawn. No. 142003 suffered minor damage and was subsequently repaired.

At privatisation, the ninety-five Class 142s were split between North Western Trains (First North Western) and Northern Spirit (MTL). In 2000, MTL ran into financial difficulties and their fleet passed to Arriva (Arriva Trains Northern). Previously, in 1998, seven units (142085–142091) were swapped for seven Class 150/2 Sprinter units from South Wales and opened up a new area of operation for the class, being deployed on the Valley Lines network operating from Cardiff Canton depot under the aegis of the Valley Lines (Cardiff Railway Company/Prism Rail) franchise. Fourteen more 142s would be sent to Cardiff in 2000, but in the event, the Valley Lines fleet would settle at fifteen units, and subsequently, six sets migrated back north.

In 2001 the Valley Lines network became part of the large Wales and Borders franchise (National Express), and then Arriva Trains Wales from 2003 until October 2018.

No. 142008 in its original Greater Manchester PTE livery was stood at Preston with a southbound ECS working on 8 August 1990. No. 142008 was damaged beyond repair and subsequently scrapped following a rear-end collision at Winsford on the WCML on 23 June 1999.

In First North Western livery, 142040 was stood at Salwick with the 11.09 Colne to Blackpool South service on 1 March 2004.

Class 142

The last Class 142 built, 142096, in Regional Railways livery with 'Arriva' branding was negotiating the sharp curve on the former Midland Railway route from Settle Junction, as it arrived at Carnforth with the 14.19 Leeds to Morecambe service on 29 March 2003.

Having been loaned to First Great Western and still retaining the obsolete First North Western dark blue livery with gold stars, minus any branding, 142068 was back home, passing Fettlers Wharf Marina at Rufford with the 13.26 Preston to Ormskirk service on 12 November 2008.

Back in 2004, the First North Western and Arriva Trains North franchises were merged into a new Northern Rail company (Serco-Abellio), the new operation having seventy-nine Class 142s in their fleet. Under the new company, the units ran for a period in their former liveries, but with a small 'Northern' brand name; however, progressively, the fleet would wear a striking livery of dark blue and purple, which transformed their appearance.

In 2007, twelve Class 142s were transferred to First Great Western (142001, 004, 009, 020 020, 062–064, 067–068, and 070), for use in Devon and Cornwall. Operating from Exeter, they acted as cover while the FGW Class 150 fleet was undergoing refurbishment and the reforming of the Class 158 units to three cars. Five Class 142s returned north in late 2008, with the remaining seven units being returned in December 2011. When they came back north, they were notable at the time as the only 142s remaining in the former 'First North Western' dark blue livery with gold stars.

In 2016, the Northern Rail franchise was replaced by Arriva Rail North, the 'Northern' branding being removed prior to the changeover. A decision was made by the new franchise that only refurbished units would carry the new Northern livery of blue and white, and consequently, with the 142s having a limited operational life, the seventy-nine units have remained in the old (de-branded) livery.

The South Wales Valley Lines fleet of fifteen units were transferred from Arriva Trains Wales to Transport for Wales (TfW) in October 2018. The new operator committed to the replacement of the fleet by the end of 2019, and during the early part of 2019, bilingual (English and Welsh) vinyl overlays appeared on the sides of the Cardiff-based fleet. Unit 142073 had been stopped for a period during late 2018 but was returned to service at Cardiff in February 2019. The TfW 142s had Department of Transport (DfT) derogation to operate until 30 July 2020, later extended to 31 December 2020.

No. 142096 was passing Cartmell Lane as it was running between Moss Side and Lytham with the 13.50 Colne to Blackpool South service on 26 February 2011.

Class 142

The view along the River Calder as 142020 was passing over Bank Top Viaduct, while it was running between Burnley Barracks and Burnley Central with the 10.57 Preston–Colne service on 15 November 2018. The 142 is in unbranded Northern livery.

One of fifteen Class 142s based at Cardiff Canton depot, 142006 was passing Cardiff East Junction with the 09.17 Bargoed to Penarth service on 21 March 2019. The unit has had multi-lingual TfW bodyside vinyl overlays placed over the now obsolete Arriva Trains Wales livery.

Into Service

In April 2019, there were seventy-nine sets working for Arriva Northern and fifteen sets working for TfW:

Operator	No. of Sets	Unit Numbers
Northern	79	142001, 142003–142005, 142007, 142009, 142011–142058, 142060–142068, 142070, 142071, 142078, 142079, 142084, 142086–142096.
TfW	15	142002, 142006, 142010, 142069, 142072–142077, 142080–142083, 142085.

All the Northern units were allocated between Heaton and Newton Heath depots. The TfW units were allocated to Cardiff Canton depot. When new, Neville Hill depot at Leeds had a sizeable allocation of 142s; eventually these would be based at Heaton depot on Tyneside.

All the Class 142s were due to be returned to the lease company, Angel Trains, by the end of 2019. The original plan was for the first batch of Northern units to be withdrawn in November 2018, with a rolling programme of withdrawals each month, with the aim of having all the 142s off the network by June 2019. In the event, late deliveries of new Class 195 DMUs, quality issues, driver training, and the cascade of Class 150/170/158 units from elsewhere in the UK, and other issues, has ensured that the 142s have had an extended period of operation. The first batch of Northern units were withdrawn in August 2019 (142005, 016, 021, 022, 025, 044, and 066). During December 2019, three Northern 142s (142012, 079, and 086) were sent to Landore depot in South Wales to act as spares donors for the fifteen TfW units. Most of the Northern fleet was retired at the end of December 2019, with a handful of units surviving in service through to February 2020. These particular examples could only work coupled to a PRM compliant unit.

The worldwide coronavirus epidemic that affected the UK in early 2020 saw a fall-off in passenger numbers across the network, and consequently, the remaining Northern and TfW 142s were placed into storage. With the lockdown restrictions easing in spring and early summer 2020, and the need for social distancing on public transport, the DfT issued derogation on 25 May 2020 that thirteen Northern 142s (142004, 018, 023, 058, 065, 068, 070, 071, 078, 087, 090, 094, and 095) could be returned to service until 31 December 2020, but only to operate with a PRM compliant unit.

Over the years, the fleet has certainly given value for money, and with Network Rail track access payments of less than 20 pence per mile, they have been cheap to operate. During the early part of 2020, many withdrawn 142s were acquired for use on heritage railways, ensuring the 'experience' of riding aboard a class 142 Pacer can be savoured for many years to come. Other less fortunate members of the Northern fleet have subsequently been scrapped, but in the main, they had the glory of being driven for some distances under their own power to the scrapyards, making one last melancholy journey and proving that they were not quite the wrecks that people perceived them to be.

The National Railway Museum acquired the doyen of the class, 142001, for the National Collection. An item of rolling stock must earn its place here as they cannot preserve everything, and despite the derision that the 142s have had during their working lives, maybe they will now be seen as the unsung heroes—at last, receiving the limelight.

5

Newton Heath Depot Maintenance

Newton Heath depot in East Manchester has been home for much of the Northern Class 142 fleet for nearly thirty-five years, with many of the units going there new and still on the allocation in 2019—a unique achievement for not only the depot but also for diesel multiple units, which generally tend to have a nomadic life.

Newton Heath was opened as a motive power depot for the Lancashire and Yorkshire Railway in 1876. Located in the 'V' of Thorpes Bridge Junction, just over 2 miles east of Manchester Victoria, it had the Calder Valley main line on one side and the Oldham Loop on the other side. The depot once had a significant allocation of locomotives, reflecting its status as one of the largest sheds on the L&Y system, its shed code being '1'. It became part of the LMS in 1923, and until 1935, the depot was coded C1, when it became 26A. During the LMS period, and after 1948, in BR days, Newton Heath had a large allocation of Stanier Class 5 4-6-0 locomotives. The depot was recoded to 9D in 1963. From the late 1950s onwards, Newton Heath was synonymous with diesel multiple units, the Cravens Class 105 Power-Twin units and the Class 104 BRCW Manchester–Blackpool 'White Liners' being the best remembered as the 1960s became the 1970s.

In April 2019, the depot allocation consisted of forty-four Class 142s, seventy-five two-car Class 150 Sprinters, and twenty-one two-car Class 156 units. Other Northern diesel units visit Newton Heath (Classes 144, 150, 153, 155, 156, and 158) for fuel and berthing as necessary between duties in the Manchester area. The depot currently employs 228 staff and is a significant employer in east Manchester. During the evening peak-time service on Thursday, 11 April 2019, at 5 p.m., forty of the forty-four Newton Heath-allocated Class 142 sets were out and about on the network, giving a fleet availability of 91 per cent, 142031, 142048, 142055, and 142062 being the only sets on the depot.

Units that are not out-stationed at other locations on the Northern network for operational purposes return home to Newton Heath every night. The last of the units are on the depot at around 2.40 a.m., and the first will be setting out for the day's duties by 4.30 a.m. While on the depot, all will be fuelled and have their coolant and lubricating oils checked and replenished where necessary. There is also an overnight cleaning team, which ensures that the units are kept tidy, inside and externally. Every sixty days, a unit will receive a deep clean to the interior. Each night, the driver's fault books are also examined, and any issues are resolved where possible before the unit returns to service.

Every 7,000 miles, units have a basic 'A' examination; at 21,000 miles, they receive a more intensive 'B' examination; while at 500,000 miles, a unit will receive a 'C4', which involves lifting the cars from the wheelsets, the whole unit in effect being given 'the works treatment'. Such procedures used to be done at a main works, but depots are now equipped to deal with such maintenance. A specific undercover road inside the main running shed at Newton Heath is set aside for 'C4' examinations. The depot has a pool of refurbished Cummins LT10-R 225-hp Diesel engines, which are overhauled every 500,000 miles of running. Refurbishment of the engines is done by Wabtec/LH Plant at Doncaster. The wheelsets are also exchanged as necessary and at a 'C4' examination. The wheelsets and the Voith Hydraulic Transmission components are also refurbished and renewed by Wabtec/LH Plant; again, the depot has a pool of refurbished wheelsets in stock. It is worth noting that although the depot at Newton Heath has a skilled workforce and a comprehensive stores facility, the original equipment manufacturers of the Class 142 components, are in the main no longer in existence, and technically, the trains are obsolete, which makes the efforts of all involved in keeping the fleet running more remarkable.

The mileage of each individual unit is monitored by the train diagrammers, based at the depot. They ensure that units are rotated on various duties to even out mileages and vary the routes that the sets work, ensuring that no particular member of the fleet has a higher mileage or is facing more attention by maintenance staff due to it having a more arduous series of diagrams (long-distance runs, high-speed running, steep gradients, frequent short-distance station stops, etc. all give wear to the components of each unit).

The 'technical incident' index (this used to be known as 'miles per casualty'), stood at 12,500 miles per unit in April 2019. The depot employs three experienced technical riding inspectors, so that if a driver, via Northern Control, flags up a specific ongoing fault on a unit that is not safety-critical, the TRI can rendezvous with the errant unit during its duties, and where possible, keep the train in service with the minimum of delay. On the depot, faults and failures are rectified, and the depot operates a 'Triage' system, in that should a unit fail for three consecutive times, it is taken out of service and stood down; it does not return to service until the problem is investigated and bottomed out.

Each 142 will give around 8 miles to the gallon of diesel fuel, but this figure is dependent on driver technique, the weather, and rail conditions. The 142 fleet is fitted with the original style toilet disposal system (i.e. the waste is discharged directly on to the track beneath the unit), but when the units are in motion, toilet waste can attach itself to the underside of the chassis and engine, creating an additional hazard for maintenance staff who need to access the underside of the units. The depot then (April 2019) had no wheel lathe, and any tyre turning or elimination of 'flats' had to rectified at either Allerton (Liverpool), Neville Hill (Leeds), or Longsight (South Manchester) depots, all of which have wheel lathes *in situ*.

During 2019, building work was ongoing at Newton Heath in preparation for the introduction of the new two- and three-car CAF-built Class 195 DMU fleet; this will at last give the depot a wheel lathe on site, and it is all part of an ongoing programme to ensure that Newton Heath will be servicing state-of-the-art diesel trains for the foreseeable future.

Class 142

Above: Nos 142062 and 142055 were stood in the yard at Newton Heath depot on 11 April 2019.

Below left: The view at frame level of the inner bar coupling between the two cars of set 142055 (55705 and 55751). The engine exhaust can be seen emerging from under the left-hand chassis, while the exhaust for the right-hand car is in the right foreground. The hose is the air connection between the two cars, while on the lower right, the oblong toilet discharge chute from the DMSL car is just visible.

Below right: A Cummins LT10-R 225-hp six-cylinder diesel engine as fitted to the 142s, awaiting collection for refurbishment. Newton Heath has a pool of refurbished engines in stock, and the depot has an engine removal pit for ease of changeover.

Newton Heath Depot Maintenance

A refurbished wheelset with part of the Voith hydraulic transmission unit on the axle.

No. 142048 stabled in the sidings at Newton Heath, in the company of Class 150/2 Sprinter 150220. As well as Class 142s, the depot has a sizeable allocation of Class 150s.

6

At Work

The South-West

With the rolling hills of North Devon as backdrop, 142027 and 142020 were departing from Umberleigh with the 16.45 Exmouth to Barnstaple service on 29 July 1987. There were thirteen 'Skipper' Class 142s sent new to Plymouth Laira depot in 1986 (142015–142027).

At Work

With the A379 on one side and the Exe Estuary on the other, 'Skippers' 142024 and 142019 were passing Cockwood, running between Starcross and Dawlish Warren with the 17.45 Exmouth to Paignton service on 27 May 1987.

At a location that once had so much railway infrastructure in the days when the former Southern Railway routes reached the North Devon towns and coastal resorts, 142026 and 142018 had reached the end of the line from Exeter, at Barnstaple on 21 July 1987. The signal at the south end of the station was showing clear, and the pair of 'Skippers' would be soon underway with the 14.26 departure to Exeter Central.

Class 142

With the Exe Estuary and the pier as a backdrop, 'Skipper' 142021 was stood at Starcross with the 16.15 Exmouth to Paignton service on 24 May 1987.

No. 142016 was almost at journey's end as it was approaching the single-track terminus at Exmouth with the 11.12 Exeter St Davids to Exmouth service on 27 May 1987. On summer Saturdays in the now far-off 1950s, the busy terminus here handled trains to London Waterloo as well as holiday traffic to and from the Midlands and the North.

At Work

Amid England's green and pleasant land, a pair of 'Skippers', 142024 and 142027, were running in fantastic evening lighting conditions, as they were departing from Umberleigh with the 18.33 Barnstaple to Exeter St Davids service on 19 July 1987.

In the glorious north Devon countryside, 142015 and 142024 were approaching Umberleigh while working the 16.45 Exmouth to Barnstaple service on 31 July 1987.

Class 142

A family with a toddler in a pushchair and two Labradors scrambled down from 142025 as it was stood with 142027 at Starcross while working the 16.35 Paignton to Exmouth service on 24 May 1987. The height of the Skipper compared to the level of the platform is noticeable here. The thirteen Skippers had only twelve months left in the West Country before all were transferred north to Newton Heath and Heaton depots, due to excessive flange and tyre wear on some of the tightly curved Cornish branches. Despite much work to fix the issues, it was decided that with such a small fleet, it was more beneficial to send them to areas where there were already 142s in quantity, and the West Country cobbled together surviving first-generation DMUs as a stopgap, until the new BREL York-built Class 150/2 Sprinter units arrived in sufficient quantities.

South Wales

With Cardiff Queen Street station in the far distance, 142083 was passing Cardiff East Junction while working the 08.33 Radyr to Penarth service, and about to pass 142082 and 142010 outbound from Cardiff Central with the 09.18 Penarth to Bargoed service on 21 March 2019. The Great Western South Wales main line is just visible on the lower right, while the 1-mile Cardiff Bay branch is in the left foreground. While all three units retain their now obsolete Arriva Trains Wales livery, all have had Transport for Wales (TfW) vinyl overlays applied to the bodysides.

At Work

With Graig Terrace as a backdrop, TfW 142072 was arriving at Pontypridd with the 12.41 Barry Island to Aberdare service on 20 March 2019. There are fifteen Class 142s allocated to Cardiff Canton depot; they are used mainly on TfW Welsh Valley Lines services.

TfW Class 142s 142085 and 142073 were stood at Pontypridd awaiting custom while working the 12.52 Aberdare to Barry Island service on 20 March 2019. Once part of the pre-grouping Taff Vale Railway, the main station platform and buildings date from 1914, and the platform visible in this view, was once the longest island platform in the world. Beyond the station, the routes to Aberdare and Treherbert go their separate ways at Pontypridd Junction.

Class 142

After crossing the 250-yard causeway from Barry Junction, 142010 was arriving at Barry Island at the conclusion of its 32-mile journey with the 14.08 departure from Merthyr Tydfil on 20 March 2019. Located on the Bristol Channel, Barry Island is still a popular holiday resort. Barry Island was once the location of a Butlin's holiday camp, opening in 1966 and closing its doors in 1996.

With a KX100 telephone kiosk on platform seven, Transport for Wales (TfW) Class 142 142006 was awaiting departure from platform eight at Cardiff Central with the 20.31 to Penarth on 19 March 2019. All the TfW Class 142 Pacer fleet have had bodyside vinyls added over the former Arriva Trains Wales livery.

At Work

No. 142002 was at platform seven at Cardiff Central with the 15.18 Penarth to Bargoed service on 19 March 2019. No. 142002 was the second of the Class 142s, built in 1985 and originally part of the Greater Manchester-liveried fleet (142001–142014). Cardiff Central was rebuilt by the GWR between 1931 and 1934; the buildings, platforms, and entrance hall are now grade II-listed structures.

Nos 142073 and 142085 were stood in the bay platform at Bridgend, awaiting departure with the 10.42 Bridgend to Aberdare service on 20 March 2019. The pair of 142s will take the coastal route on the Vale of Glamorgan line, via Cardiff International Airport, Barry and Cadoxton to Cardiff Central, while Class 150/2 Sprinter 150264 was departing with the 10.16 Maesteg to Cardiff Central service, taking the more direct route along the former GWR South Wales main line.

Class 142

Cardiff architecture old and new as the tail end of 142081 was passing over West Canal Wharf as it entered Cardiff Central with the 07.38 Merthyr Tydfil to Bridgend service on 21 March 2019. The Glamorganshire Canal once ran along here. The canal ran from Merthyr Tydfil to Cardiff with fifty-two locks *en route*. It was completed in 1794, and the last section was closed in 1951. As here, most of the canal has been redeveloped, filled-in, or abandoned entirely. This street location was once used for a scene in the BBC television series *Doctor Who*, the street and bridge being featured in a 2006 episode entitled 'Love and Monsters'.

Nos 142073 and 142085 were joining the Vale of Glamorgan line at Barry Junction, as they came off the short branch from Barry Island while forming the 17.41 Barry Island to Pontypridd service on 20 March 2019. The station appears to have some original GWR platform seats.

At Work

Against a backdrop of new development, 142010 and 142082 were approaching Cardiff Central with the 08.26 Merthyr Tydfil to Barry Island service on a damp 21 March 2019.

Yorkshire and Lincolnshire

In its original BR Provincial Services blue livery, 142076 was arriving at the market town of Skipton with a Leeds to Morecambe service on 18 July 1988. This view has since been totally transformed with re-signalling and the Aire Valley electrification from Leeds Bradford to Skipton completed in 1994.

Class 142

In Regional Railways livery, 142076 was departing from Hellifield with the 14.17 Leeds to Morecambe service on 4 March 2000.

High in the Yorkshire Dales National Park, 142079 and 156489 were stood at Ribblehead station while working the 16.27 Carlisle to Leeds service on 28 May 1997. The 112-mile journey from the border city of Carlisle to Leeds, via the former Midland Railway S&C line, would take just under three hours. Class 142s have never been common visitors to the route.

At Work

No. 142064 was stabled between duties at Huddersfield on 29 September 2012. The 142 was stood adjacent to the former London and North Western Railway goods warehouse with its disused wagon lift.

No. 142020 had just left the stabling sidings adjacent to Sheffield station and was awaiting clearance to enter the platform to form the 14.14 departure to Manchester Piccadilly on 6 October 2012. The 142s have been regular performers on the Hope Valley route between Manchester and Sheffield for many years.

Class 142

Eager Saturday shoppers were heading for the delights of the Meadowhall Shopping Centre as 142091 was preparing to depart with the 13.06 Sheffield to Leeds service on 17 March 2012. Located 3 miles north-east of Sheffield city centre, the Meadowhall Shopping Centre opened in 1990 and is currently the only shopping centre complex in the UK that has a transport interchange. Located near to junction 34 on the M1 motorway, the centre is served by National Rail services and the Sheffield Supertram network; it also has a bus interchange.

Running over newly laid track, 142015 was arriving at South Milford with the 14.13 Selby to Huddersfield service on 3 May 2014. No. 142015 was originally the first of the Devon and Cornwall 'Skipper' units.

At Work

No. 142022 was getting underway from Selby with the 11.05 Hull to York service, while in the bay platform, Class 158 158755 was awaiting departure with the 12.44 to Wakefield Westgate on 29 September 2012. Until 1981, Selby was located on the East Coast Main Line.

In unbranded Northern livery, 142021 was passing the semaphore signals at Crabley Creek level crossing while working the 11.42 Doncaster to Hull service on 6 May 2017.

Class 142

No. 142054 was departing from Hull with a well-patronised 12.03 departure to York on 21 September 2013. The 142 was one of the former Merseytravel batch of seventeen units given revised seating and larger dot-matrix destination panels in 1992.

On the electrified Leeds to Doncaster route, 142007 was stood at Adwick Interchange with the 15.24 Adwick to Sheffield (via Doncaster) service on 11 August 2018. Adwick is the turn-back point for Doncaster and Sheffield stopping services. When new, 142007 was once part of the batch of Greater Manchester PTE orange and brown units (142001–142014).

At Work

No. 142015 was departing from Doncaster with the 08.36 Beverley to Sheffield service on 11 August 2018. With a reversal at Hull *en route*, the total distance is 74 miles.

At a location that was once busy with coal traffic in the days when the three nearby power stations of Drax, Eggborough, and Ferrybridge were supplied twenty-four hours a day with MGR trains, 142027 was arriving at a now quieter Knottingley with the 13.17 Leeds to Knottingley service on 17 September 2017. Following a reversal at nearby England Lane, the 142 would form the 14.26 Knottingley to Leeds service.

Class 142

Northern Class 142 Pacers at rest under the overall roof at York station on 15 June 2019. In the foreground, sister units 142063 and 142064 were stabled at platform seven, while across at platform one was 142078, which would eventually work the 13.15 York to Sheffield service. No. 142064 would eventually deputise for a three-car Class 158 on the 17.12 York to Blackpool North—a choice that raised a few eyebrows on its lengthy cross-Pennine journey via Leeds on a busy Saturday evening.

The view across the rooftops at Todmorden, as 142042 was crossing Todmorden viaduct with the 12.24 Wigan Wallgate to Blackburn service on 14 November 2018. The 142 will have run a circuitous journey from Wigan via Swinton and Manchester Victoria, taking the Calder Valley line to Hall Royd Junction just east of Todmorden, and running over Copy Pit Summit to reach the East Lancashire line at Gannow Junction, west of Burnley, and onwards to its destination at the former Cotton town of Blackburn—a total distance of 57 miles.

At Work

With both units in Tyne and Wear PTE livery, 142018 and 142021 were passing Sleights with a service from Whitby to Middlesborough on 16 July 1997. (*Courtesy Roger Sutcliffe*)

No. 142092 was stood at the rural station at Long Preston with the 14.29 Lancaster/Morecambe to Leeds service (74 miles) on 29 May 2016. The village of Long Preston is a small hamlet straddled along the busy A65 Trunk Road.

Class 142

No. 142025 was arriving at Barnetby with the 15.20 Cleethorpes to Sheffield service on 6 September 2014. The service was one of three 'parliamentary' workings to call at the stations between Wrawby Junction and Gainsborough on Saturdays only. The semaphore signalling at Barnetby was decommissioned in late December 2015, when control was passed to the York ROC.

No. 142070 was at platform three at the seaside terminus at Cleethorpes, with the 15.20 departure to Sheffield on 30 August 2014. On platform two is doyen of Class 153 single-unit 153301 with the 17.00 to Barton–On–Humber, while on platform one, Transpennine Express Class 185 185133 was garnering passengers for the 15.26 departure to Manchester Airport.

At Work

With traffic waiting at the level crossing on Bigby High Road, 142086 was accelerating away from the small market town of Brigg with the Saturdays only 13.28 Sheffield to Cleethorpes service on 2 December 2017. The impressive wooden-gated level crossing controlled by the adjacent signal box was then the largest traditional mechanical-style level crossing still in operation on the UK network.

No. 142063 was passing through the disused platforms of Brocklesby Junction while working the 12.00 Sheffield to Cleethorpes service on 26 May 2012. The station at Brocklesby Junction closed in October 1993. The ornate former station buildings on the up platform survive as a private residence. Just out of sight in front of the 142 is the junction with the freight-only connection to Immingham Docks and Lindsey Oil Refinery, ensuring that Brocklesby Junction is still a busy location for freight movements. They were replaced by lifting barriers in March 2020.

Under a threatening sky, 142090 had just crossed the A18 as it departed from Althorpe with the 13.19 Scunthorpe to Lincoln Central service on 19 November 2016. Running via Doncaster and Sheffield, this was a 90-mile, two-hour-and-forty-four-minute Class 142 marathon.

The North-West

An eight-car rake (four sets) of Class 142s, with Greater Manchester 142004 leading, were passing Kirkham North Junction while running empty stock from Blackpool North to Preston on 24 September 1988. The train contains all three initial livery variations of the Class 142 fleet.

At Work

Funicular-style, PTE-liveried Class 142s were passing while forming the early morning stopping service in both directions at Salwick on 5 September 2001. With both units branded 'First North Western', Revised Greater Manchester PTE 142011 was departing with a Blackpool South to Colne service, while revised Merseyrail-liveried 142046 was arriving with a Colne to St Annes-on-the-Sea working. Despite the best intentions to keep these PTE-liveried units within their original intended boundaries (Greater Manchester and Merseyside respectively), diagramming of units on varied duties to even out mileages etc., resulted in scenes such as this.

A shortage of serviceable units at Newton Heath in 2004 saw the appearance of a South Wales 'Valley Lines' liveried 142069 in the north-west for several weeks. On loan from Cardiff Canton depot, it was employed regularly on the busy hourly services on the Blackpool South–Preston–Blackburn–Accrington–Colne corridor. The colourful unit was stood at Bamber Bridge with the 15.00 Blackpool South to Colne service on 12 April 2004.

Class 142

In 'Northern Spirit' livery, 142065 was arriving at Carnforth with the 14.19 Leeds to Morecambe service on 4 September 1999. No. 142065 was the first 142 to be painted in this short-lived livery style.

With electrification work in progress, 142031 was awaiting departure from Thatto Heath with the 13.01 Liverpool Lime Street to Wigan North Western service on 18 April 2014.

Substituting for a Class 319, unbranded Northern Class 142s 142039 and 142056 were getting underway from Edge Hill with the 13.31 Wigan North Western to Liverpool Lime Street service on 25 March 2017. The Pacers have a backdrop that forms part of the oldest operational railway station in the world, the buildings here dating from 1836.

No. 142055 was arriving at Wigan Wallgate with the 10.44 Kirkby to Blackburn service on 20 April 2018. The large dot-matrix destination display is a legacy from refurbishment by Merseytravel in 1992.

Class 142

The peace and quiet of Station Road at Hoghton was momentarily disturbed as 142039 passed through the automatic half-barrier level crossing as it was running between Bamber Bridge and Pleasington while working the 09.57 Preston to Colne service on 27 July 2018.

No 142042 was approaching Blackburn with the 10.57 Preston to Colne service on 9 August 2018. Class 142s have been regular performers on the Preston to Colne route since new.

At Work

Having made its last call at Ramsgreave and Wilpshire, 142044 was easing downgrade towards Daisyfield Junction on the east side of Blackburn, passing over Cobwall Viaduct with the 09.25 Clitheroe to Rochdale service on 25 June 2018.

No. 142037 was passing over the last few arches of the nineteen-arch Accrington Viaduct while working the 13.24 Burnley Central to Preston service on 3 August 2018.

Class 142

Nos 142033 and 142042 were reaching journey's end as they were running into platform two at Manchester Piccadilly with the 15.14 departure from Rose Hill Marple on 19 April 2019. As with the Class 101 first-generation DMU fleet that was withdrawn in 2003, the routes from Manchester Piccadilly to Sheffield, New Mills Central, Marple, and Rose Hill have become regular final haunts for the Class 142 fleet.

Doyen of Class 142, 142001 was stood at the small single-track terminus at Rose Hill Marple, awaiting departure with the 14.14 to Manchester Piccadilly on 19 April 2019. Located on a short 2-mile spur from Marple Wharf Junction, the line to Rose Hill was once part of a through route to Macclesfield that was closed west of Marple in 1970.

At Work

No. 142001 was departing from New Mills Central with the 09.14 Sheffield to Manchester Piccadilly service, passing 142029 in the reversing siding on 19 April 2019. No. 142029 had worked the 09.20 departure from Manchester Piccadilly and, following arrival at New Mills, ran ECS into the siding to allow the 09.40 Piccadilly to Sheffield service to pass before working back to Manchester with the 10.26 departure from New Mills Central.

On the former Cheshire Lines Committee (CLC) route between Liverpool and Manchester, 142049 was getting underway from Urmston with the 11.55 Liverpool Lime Street to Manchester Oxford Road service on 11 September 2018. The former station building in the foreground is now a bar and restaurant. In 1986, when new, 142049 visited Canada and was an exhibit at expo86 in Vancouver.

Class 142

In evening light, 142023 was departing from Bolton with the 18.25 Clitheroe to Rochdale service on 21 August 2018. The former Lancashire and Yorkshire iron and glass platform canopies have been retained at Bolton.

Nos 142061 and 142009 were running alongside Midland Way as they were approaching Warrington Central with a Liverpool Lime Street to Manchester Oxford Road service on 9 April 2011.

At Work

No. 142036 and a Class 150/2 Sprinter were starting out from platform four at Southport with the 13.45 departure to Clitheroe on 3 June 2018. In the foreground, Merseyrail EMUs 508143 and 507005 were stabled for the weekend, while just visible on platform three is 508138 awaiting departure with the 13.58 Northern Line service to Liverpool South Parkway.

No. 142036 was crossing the River Lune at Lancaster with the 4-mile 15.27 Lancaster to Morecambe shuttle service on 6 April 2019.

Class 142

On the last day of 2018 and looking as though it was in a walled garden, 142049 was stood at Lytham while working the 11.13 Blackpool South to Preston service.

Cumbria and the North-East

In ex-works, unbranded, and revised Greater Manchester livery, 142062 was arriving at Foxfield on the Cumbrian Coast Line, with the 13.03 Carlisle to Preston service on 29 May 1997. The 142 will have passed along the long and winding route that follows the coast and is the slower, less direct way between Carlisle, South Cumbria, and North Lancashire. The nuclear facility at Sellafield has ensured the future of this scenic railway. Foxfield was once the junction station for trains on the branch to Coniston; it closed to passengers in 1958 and freight in 1962. No. 142062 was a long way from its home depot at Newton Heath in East Manchester.

At Work

On an overcast afternoon, Greater Manchester-liveried 142012 was departing from Ravenglass with the 13.03 Carlisle to Preston service on 30 May 1996. In the background is the terminus of the 15-inch gauge Ravenglass and Eskdale Railway. Visible at the far end of the car park are the two vintage Pullman cars *Elmira* and *Maid of Kent*, in use as camping coaches and holiday lets.

No. 142067 was setting out of bay platform five at the border city of Carlisle at the commencement of its 61-mile journey with the 11.35 to Newcastle on 11 February 2017.

Class 142

With the distant signal for nearby Milton Gates showing clear, 142021 was leaning into the curve as it departed from Brampton with the 108-mile 15.28 Carlisle to Middlesborough service on 8 October 2016.

No. 142086 was arriving at Haltwhistle with the 08.31 Carlisle to Newcastle service on 8 October 2016. Haltwhistle was once the junction station for the 13.5-mile branch to Alston that closed in May 1976.

At Work

No. 142092 was stood under the overall roof at Newcastle Central, garnering passengers while forming the 78-mile, 08.50 Carlisle to Morpeth service on 7 September 2019.

Amid the autumn tints in the trees, 142021 was approaching Bardon Mill while working the 12.23 Newcastle to Carlisle service on 8 October 2016.

Class 142

Nos 142066 and 142022 were departing from the small station at Newton Aycliffe with the 10.17 Bishop Auckland to Saltburn service on 16 February 2014. The station was opened at Newton Aycliffe by BR in 1978.

With the North Eastern Railway overall roof as a backdrop, 142094 was stood at Darlington on 10 October 2018. The 142 had worked the 08.44 from Saltburn to Darlington, and should have gone on to Bishop Auckland, but following an incident between Redcar and Middlesborough, the service was terminated at Darington, forming the 10.40 departure back to Saltburn.

At Work

No. 142023 was awaiting custom at Thornaby while working the 74-mile 12.19 Nunthorpe to Hexham service on 10 October 2018.

With the transporter bridge visible on the horizon, 142094 was arriving at Middlesbrough with the 13.11 Bishop Auckland to Salburn service on 10 October 2018.

Class 142

Against a backdrop of industrial Teesside, 142065 was approaching Middlesbrough with the 14.11 Bishop Auckland to Saltburn service on 10 October 2018.

Surrounded by the closed steelworks at Redcar, 142088 had departed from the small station at South Bank with the 15.11 Bishop Auckland to Saltburn service, while coming in other direction was Freightliner Class 66 66957, with the 16.12 Tees Dock to Felixstowe intermodal service on 10 October 2018. South Bank station once gave direct access to one of the entrance gates of the large and sprawling steel works complex.

At Work

No. 142088 was arriving at the staggered platform layout at South Bank while working the 16.42 Saltburn to Bishop Auckland service on 10 October 2018. The scene is dominated by the redundant Redcar Steelworks. Once the second-largest steel plant in Europe, the former Dorman Long works closed in 2015. In the past, Redcar supplied steel for the Sydney Harbour Bridge, the Tyne Bridge, and the Auckland Harbour Bridge in New Zealand.

No. 142093 was stood at Saltburn-by-the-Sea, awaiting departure from the small terminus with 14.34 departure to Bishop Auckland on 9 October 2018. The line to the seaside resort was opened by the Stockton and Darlington Railway from Redcar in August 1861.

Class 142

At Work

Looking quite insignificant, 142022 was crossing the River Tyne on Stephenson's 1849 1,338-foot-long high-level bridge, while running towards Newcastle East Junction with the 69-mile, 10.35 Middlesborough to Hexham service on 7 September 2019.

Opposite above: The shops on Milton Street form a backdrop to 142023 as it was stood at Saltburn-by-the-Sea with the 16.17 departure to Darlington on 9 October 2018.

Opposite below: On a damp Autumn morning, 142094 was awaiting departure from Redcar Central while forming the 08.44 Saltburn to Bishop Auckland service on 11 October 2018. Meanwhile, Arriva North East, Temsa single-deck bus 4724/YJ11 GHD on route sixty-three was passing over the level crossing that takes West Dyke Road over the railway. Controlled from the adjacent signal box, the level crossing is protected by telescopic metal gates that were installed in 2015 and are unique to Redcar Central.

7
Interiors

The interior of the DMSL 55598 of 142007 on 11 August 2018. The car has retained its original Leyland National bus-type seating in 'three plus two' unidirectional configuration, albeit trimmed in Northern blue moquette. The lavatory compartment is at the far end on the right side adjacent to the gangway between the two cars.

Interiors

Above: Looking towards the cab and entrance doors of DMSL 55598 of 142007, with the single luggage rack at roof height, and the small three-a-side seats opposite each other adjacent to the doors. No. 142007 was one of the units that had the interiors 'facelifted' by First North Western.

Right: The gangway end of 55598 (142007), showing the side door and the view through to DMS car 55548. The emergency wooden ladder is strapped to the bulkhead, while the small open yellow litter bin is adjacent to the gangway. This view also shows the passenger-operated 'Door Open/Door Close' buttons mounted on the vertical handrail adjacent to the doors. The toilet compartment is off view to the immediate right.

Class 142

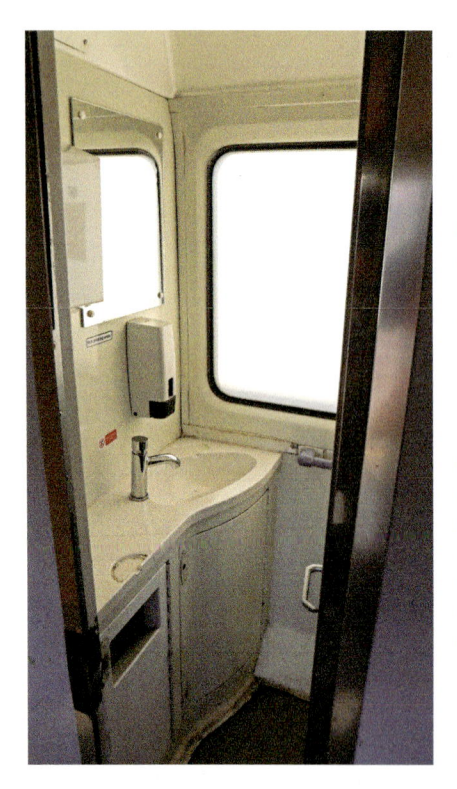

Left: The small toilet compartment of DMS 55598 (142007). The washbasin, vanity unit, and litter bin are the original fitments manufactured in glass-reinforced plastic. The toilet is out of view behind the door. The 142s do not have toilet retention tanks; once flushed, the contents discharge directly on to the track.

Below: The view looking forwards to the cab door of DMS 55548 (142007), with a luggage rack and bike storage area on the right-hand side, with a tip-up side seat on the opposite side of the gangway, that can be utilised as a wheelchair space. The disabled ramp is located against the bulkhead at this end of the car. When built, the end space had three-a-side seating facing inwards on each side, and there was a glass and steel bulkhead with a lockable door, dividing the end space to the main passenger saloon, so that mail and parcels could be carried securely at one end of the car. With the cessation of such traffic, the doors were all eventually removed.

Interiors

The interior of former Merseytravel DMSL 55636 (142045). Looking from behind the cab door, the original seating in the main saloon was replaced with low back 'three plus two' seating, all facing the same direction and having integral hand grips. The original three-a-side seats were retained by the doorway. These units (142041–142049 and 142051–142058) also had a small dot-matrix destination display mounted above the gangway at the cab end of each car, the rear of which is visible at roof height adjacent to the partition.

Detail of the rear open rear doors of DMSL 55637 (142046). The toilet area is behind the orange door, the first step with its built-in lighting that illuminates when the doors open even in daylight, with the Northern network map mounted on the toilet partition wall. The passenger-operated push buttons for opening the doors are located either side of the door partitions; the outer bead of the button surround illuminates only when the doors are in the 'open' mode. On the lower right is the emergency door release handle encased behind a glass panel. The roof seems to have sealant applied to some of the body module joints.

Class 142

The former Northern Spirit/Arriva Trains North 142s had the original seating replaced by high-backed individual 'two plus two' seats that were unidirectional in rows. This is the interior of DMSL 55790 (142094) on 10 October 2018. The car has two head-height longitudinal luggage racks.

No. 142002 started life as a Greater Manchester PTE unit with 'three plus two' bus-type seating, but it is now part of the former Arriva Trains Wales (now TfW) fleet based at Cardiff. All the units have been upgraded internally with individual high-backed Chapman seating, and there is a revised seating arrangement and wheelchair space at the saloon ends by the entrance doors. More prominent passenger door operation buttons have also been fitted. Only one overhead luggage rack is fitted. This was DMSL 55593 of set 142002 on 20 March 2019.

Interiors

Above: The driver's side cab details of 142055.

Right: The offside of the driving cab with tip-up seat, 142055.

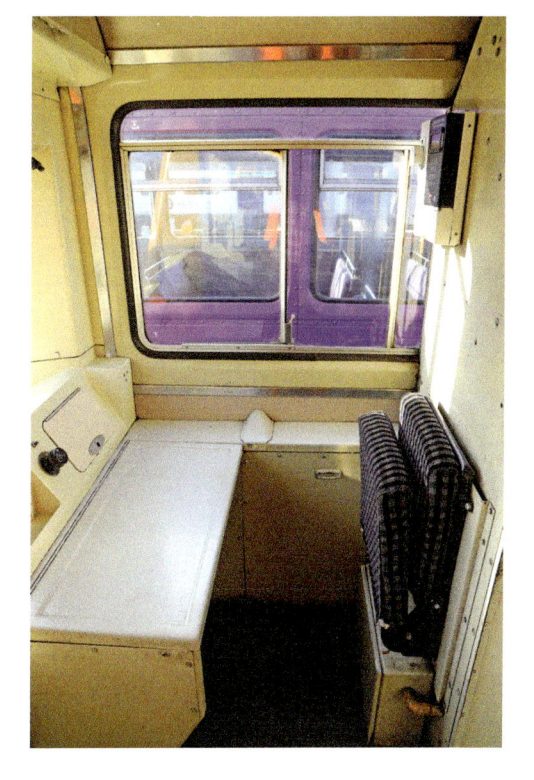

8

A 142 Miscellany

Above left: A 142 had a starring role in a Northern/Community Rail Lancashire poster in 2017.

Above right: A collectable of the future?

A 142 Miscellany

A painted mural of Bamber Bridge, displayed at Bamber Bridge station and completed by local schoolchildren, has a class 142 as part of the time-related scene.

All the fives as 142014 was departing from Rainford Junction with DMS 55555 at the rear, forming the 10.14 Manchester Victoria to Kirkby service on 27 September 2016.

Class 142

The view from Station Close at Rishton as 142028 was rolling to halt with the 11.57 Preston to Colne service on 30 January 2019.

No. 142062.

A 142 Miscellany

The interior notices and passenger operated door open and close buttons of 142035 on 21 January 2020.

A lone photographer was recording 142028 as it disappeared into Blackburn tunnel, departing from a snowy Blackburn with the 10.57 Preston to Colne service on 25 January 2019. Ignored by many enthusiasts, interest in the Pacer fleet was growing as they became an endangered species.

Class 142

Against the setting sun, 142036 was running along the WCML at Penwortham, south of Preston, with the 19.20 Preston to Ormskirk service on 12 April 2012.

In a rural setting, the pioneer Class 142, 142001 was heading into a setting sun on New Year's Day, 1 January 2019. The unit was working the 15.26 Preston to Ormskirk service passing Broadfield Farm, while running between Midge Hall and Croston. Over thirty years since it was new, 142001 and its surviving classmates were still in service, long beyond their projected lifespan; unfortunately, time has caught up with these unsung workhorses, and scenes such as this along here are now gone forever.

9

Scale Models

The Class 142 was first replicated in 00/1:76 scale by Hornby, with the first versions being available in model shops in 1987. It was a well-detailed model for its time, with some 5,000 rivets being replicated on the plastic-moulded bodyshells. The first few issues had motors fitted in both cars; this was later dropped, and a single motor with improved current collection to give smoother running qualities was fitted to the model. From 1987 until 1998, the models were produced by Hornby in their Margate factory, and from 1999 onwards, production was moved to China. The tooling detail replicates the earlier bus-type doors and is incorrect for later livery versions. The model was still attractive and featured well-applied livery details. Twelve different versions were produced as per the table below.

Catalogue Number	Livery	Set Number	Availability	Notes
R867	Provincial Services Blue	142048	1987–1992	
R297	Greater Manchester Orange	142013	1989	
R326	Devon and Cornwall (Skipper)	142015	1992–1993	
R103	Regional Railways	142023	1994–1995	
R346	Tyne and Wear	142020	1995–1996	(Train Set)
R451	GM/Regional Railways	142069	1996–1997	
R1022	Northern Spirit	142065	1999	(Special Edition)
R2161	Northern Spirit	142074	2000–2002	
R2611	Merseyrail / Northern	142045	2007–2008	
R2700	Arriva Blue	142090	2008–2009	
R2809	First Great Western	142068	2010–2011	
R3140	Northern Rail	142026	2012	

Class 142

A Hornby R2611 Class 142 in revised Merseyrail livery with Northern branding, 142045 showing 'Manchester Oxford Road' on the destination displays, which was available in 2007 and 2008.

Dapol 'N' gauge ND-116D in Arriva Trains Wales livery.

Scale Models

An 'N' gauge (1:148 scale) scale model was released by Dapol Ltd during 2019. The models are super detailed state-of-the-art versions, featuring working directional lights, with digital DCC versions being available. The first issues were as per the table below.

Catalogue Number	Livery	Set Number	Notes
ND116A	Northern Rail	142065	DCC version is NS116AD
ND116B	Regional Railways	142081	DCC version is ND116BD
ND116C	Northern Spirit	142025	DCC version is ND116CD
ND116D	Arriva Trains Wales	142085	DCC version is ND116DD
ND116E	Tyne and Wear PTE	142021	DCC version is ND116ED

Bibliography

Bridge, M., *Track Atlas of Mainland Britain* 2nd Edition (Sheffield: Platform 5 Publishing, 2012)
Butcher, A. C., *The Heyday of the DMU* (Weybridge: Ian Allan Ltd, 1994)
Haresnape, B., *British Rail Fleet Survey 8 First Generation DMUs* (Weybridge: Ian Allan Ltd, 1985)
Haresnape, B., *British Rail Fleet Survey 9 Second Generation DMUs* (Weybridge: Ian Allan Ltd, 1986)
Sales Brochure—BRE-Leyland Railbus (Leyland Vehicles/BREL, 1984)
Tufnell, R. M., *The British Railcar AEC to HST* (Newton Abbot: David and Charles, 1984)